STOTT PARK
BOBBIN MILL

CUMBRIA

Peter White

BA FSA

Stott Park Bobbin Mill lies deep in a wooded valley of the Lake District on the western shore of Winder-mere, near the village of Finsthwaite. One of over seventy such mills throughout Lakeland during the nineteenth century, it is a factory in miniature, having been purpose built in 1835. It was one of the last to survive, closing in 1971. Located to use the energy of the fast flowing streams to power their waterwheels, the mills drew their raw material from the surrounding coppiced woodlands, which provided the poles to be turned on the lathes.

Bobbins were essential for the large, highly mechanised Lancashire cotton spinning mills, each one of which needed many thousands to sustain production. But by the end of the nineteenth century, the cotton mills started to use cheaper substitutes and those bobbin mills that survived did so by diversifying, producing cotton reels, tool handles and spout bobbins for drainpipes.

Stott Park Bobbin Mill can be seen today little changed from its appearance a century ago.

❖ CONTENTS ❖

5 TOUR OF THE MILL
5 THE MILL BUILDINGS: EXTERIOR
7 TICKET OFFICE
9 OLD MILL: GROUND FLOOR
9 ENGINE ROOM
10 NEW LATHE SHOP
14 OLD LATHE SHOP
16 THE MILL GROUNDS
17 THE MILL'S SURROUNDINGS
17 *High Dam*
19 *Finsthwaite village*

20 HISTORY
20 BOBBINS AND THE TEXTILE INDUSTRY
22 OWNERS OF THE MILL
22 THE FIRST BOBBIN MASTERS
23 THE COWARD FAMILY
26 THE WORKPEOPLE
27 NEW PRODUCTS
28 CLOSURE

28 *Acknowledgements*
PLAN *inside back cover*

Published by English Heritage
1 Waterhouse Square,
138-142 Holborn
London EC1N 2ST
© English Heritage 2002
First published by English Heritage 2002
Reprinted 2004, 2008, 2011
Revised reprint 2013, 2013
Photography by English Heritage Photographic Unit and
copyright English Heritage unless otherwise stated.
Edited by Katy Carter. Designed by Derek Lee.
Plans by Richard Morris

Printed in England by the Pureprint Group
C20 10/13 00009 ISBN 978 1 85074 796 3
Visit our website at www.english-heritage.org.uk

To Finsthwaite village

MILLPOND
The header pond for
the water turbine

BOILER HOUSE
With drying rooms above

SMITHY
Housed a hearth,
with lofts for drying
the part-finished
bobbins above

STOTT PARK
HAMLET
Provided accommodation
for mill workers

Stott Park Bobbin Mill
Low Stott Park
Ulverston
Cumbria
LA12 8AZ
01539 531087

BIRD'S-EYE VIEW OF THE MILL

Overflow car park

DRYING SHEDS
Provided additional space for drying out the bobbins

OLD MILL
The original two-storey building of 1835; the lathes were on the upper floor and powered by a waterwheel on the far side

Way in and ticket office

COPPICE BARN
Used to store and season timber; now houses an exhibition about the mill

NEW LATHE SHOP
Built by the 1880s to expand the capacity of the mill

Car park

To Lakeside

ILLUSTRATION BY PETER DUNN

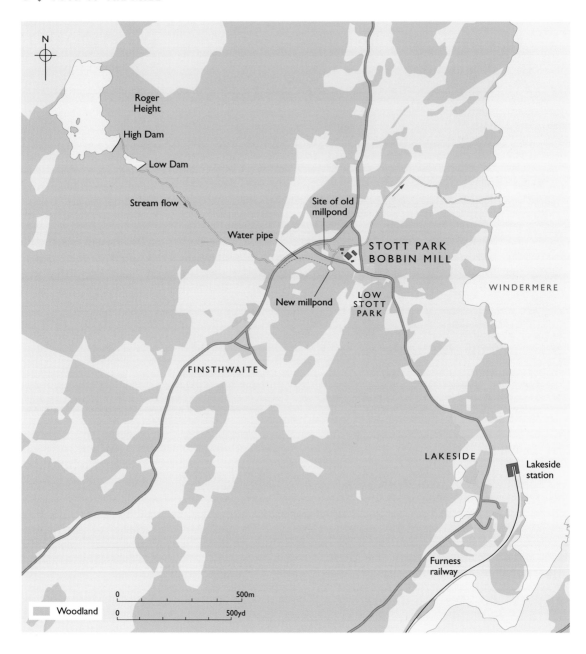

TOUR OF THE MILL

All visitors to the mill interior must join a guided tour, so you should first check the earliest available time for your tour at the ticket office. When you have done so, return to the area between the car park and the mill buildings, and look into the mill yard.

THE MILL BUILDINGS: EXTERIOR

The buildings that comprise the mill were mostly constructed by the 1880s and have changed little since then. The large, single-storey **New Lathe Shop**

Opposite: The mill and its surroundings

❖ WHAT ARE BOBBINS? ❖

Bobbins are small cylinders of wood with ends or flanges to retain yarn, wire, or any commodity that can be wound on to them. The Lakeland bobbin industry developed because millions of bobbins were needed for yarn initially in the mechanised spinning process, and it is for this reason that what was essentially a wood turning industry became known as the bobbin industry. As time went on there were hundreds of patterns, and as the mills diversified from the 1860s there were many different products.

The early bobbins were made up from three parts – the two flanges were glued to the barrel. The lathes introduced in the mid-nineteenth century, being faster and more accurate, produced bobbins and reels turned from one piece of wood.

This late nineteenth-century engraving shows a bobbin manufacturer's display of the huge variety of bobbins then being made

The Smithy had a hearth on the ground floor and lofts above, where half-finished bobbins could be dried

Some cottages in Low Stott Park housed bobbin mill workers

for the engine's boiler is prominent behind the lathe shop. The gable end of the boiler house, with timber drying rooms above, can be seen between the lathe shop roof and the chimneystack.

The **Old Mill** is the original, two-storey mill building of 1835. Its gable end is hidden by the shelter for the large circular saw which was installed much later. Note that the power for the saw comes from a belt driven by a large pulley in the gable end of the New Lathe Shop; all the machines at Stott Park, as in most nineteenth-century factories, were powered from a single source in this way. In the Old Mill, the lathes were on the upper floor of the building, behind the windows, and power came from the massive waterwheel at the far end.

The small, detached building in the yard is the **Smithy**. It housed a hearth on the ground floor and lofts for drying the part-finished bobbins above.

On the opposite side of the road a group of houses, which originated as farm buildings, were adapted and extended to house bobbin mill workers.

Enclosing the yard on the right is a **coppice barn** – there was formerly another similar one at the far end of the yard. These barns were used to store and season timber; their exact date is not known but they were very common in the area during the nineteenth century. The surviving coppice barn now houses material

(see plan at the end of the guide) is one of the most recent buildings. It was constructed as part of the mill's expansion, and housed some of the heavier, higher-speed lathes, which were powered by either the turbine or the 'new' steam engine. The chimney

❖ COPPICE BARNS ❖

Coppice barns are a characteristic building type of the Lakeland area. A roof, generally covered with Westmorland slate, is supported on a series of stone-built piers. These pillars are square at Stott Park, but in earlier examples they would have been circular. The resulting open-sided structure, similar to the familiar, metal-framed Dutch barn, provided shelter from the rain for the coppiced poles, while at the same time allowing a good circulation of air, to assist seasoning and prevent rot.

The surviving coppice barn at Stott Park, where the wood could be stored and dried out before being worked into bobbins

about the history of the mill and the families who owned it and worked there. If you now enter this building, you will find information about the mill, its people, origins, and products, providing a background for your tour. From here, you will be guided along the same route as the timber poles, when they were turned into bobbins.

TICKET OFFICE

The ticket office area was once occupied by benches for the circular saws used to cut 'cakes' or bobbin-length pieces from the poles before they were put on to the lathes. Immediately beyond the ticket office a door leads into the enclosed wheel pit (not open to view), which originally housed a 24ft diameter breast-shot waterwheel, the power source for all the machines in the original mill of 1835. The wheel was replaced by a turbine in about 1858, and the present turbine in the pit dates from 1931. You will be able to see it more clearly at the end of the tour. The power supply for the mill is described in detail on page 18.

❖ HOW ARE BOBBINS MADE? ❖

1 Coppice poles are brought from the coppice barns where they are stored, and cut to manageable lengths on circular saws

2 Poles of thicker diameter are blocked – several cylinders or blocks are bored out from each length, which is called a cake. Poles of thinner diameter are used as they are

3 The blocks, while still wet, have a hole bored through their length. This enables them to be fitted on to a roughing lathe, where the barrel and end flanges are created as the wood is turned

4 The roughs are dried, by spreading them on the perforated floors of the drying rooms

5 The holes are rinced or reemered out to clean them, and then the roughs are finished to the desired pattern on a finishing lathe

6 Finally, the bobbins are placed in a rotating drum with paraffin wax to polish them

OLD MILL: GROUND FLOOR

Moving to your left, you will enter the lower floor of the Old Mill. Note how poorly lit it is. Here, apart from the men using circular saws, young boys would have worked glueing the parts of the bobbins together, because the early lathes could not make them in one piece. Later, after the New Lathe Shop had been built, the machine to cut blocks or small cylinders of wood was located here. Several blocks were cut from each cake. These machines, which will be demonstrated to you, are all driven by belting from the line-shaft pulleys, above.

ENGINE ROOM

A doorway leads through into the New Lathe Shop, which was added by the 1880s. Just before it, a small doorway to your right leads into the Engine Room, also constructed during the period of the mill's expansion. Here is a steam engine of the simplest type, and the idea seems to have been that it would supplement the water power of the turbine. This would be necessary for at least two reasons. In the first place, the 'modern' lathes were heavier and faster, and were economically attractive because they could turn bobbins in one piece instead of three. Secondly, a consistent supply of water is necessary for power, and during the summer months, when there is most daylight, there is least water.

Left: The blocking machine on the ground floor of the Old Mill

The steam engine, built by Bradleys of Brighouse. The engine's boiler was fuelled by timber off-cuts, shavings and turnings

An iron, fireproof door opens from the new lathe shop into the stokehole for the engine's boiler. The original boiler drove the engine until the early 1950s, but it is no longer used at pressure. The engine is now kept in steam by a vertical cross-tube donkey boiler, installed in 1991 in a boiler house at the rear of the mill.

The New Lathe Shop, built to house additional lathes to expand capacity

NEW LATHE SHOP

Returning to the New Lathe Shop, notice how crowded it seems, with the machines, or lathes – where possible located near the windows for maximum light – the unguarded belts from the line-shaft pulleys, the small timber blocks in baskets or swills

A semi-automatic boring machine in use

being processed, and the piles of shavings and turnings on the floor. All the lathes were driven from the line shaft above, and when they are demonstrated, you will experience the special noise and vibration of this type of working environment. The lathe shop was a hazardous place to work (see page 14).

As you pass through the lathe shop various machines will be demonstrated. On your left, fixed to wooden beds, are the boring and rincing machines, which respectively bored the holes through the blocks and cleaned them out as part of the finishing process. The original turning lathes were of iron and fixed to timber beds like this. The boring processes involved holding the block against the revolving drill bit, and if

the wood split a hand injury could quickly result.

To your right are the **turning lathes**. They were also unguarded and again, if the timber split, pieces could fly in any direction, and injure the operator. Dust created in the lathe shop was a constant hazard throughout the mill, and workers were very prone to respiratory illness. If that was not enough, the ever-growing piles of shavings posed a fire risk, and many mills were burnt out as a result. The rapid action of the **roughing lathe**, used to shape the blocks before they were taken in swill baskets to drying rooms in preparation for the finishing processes, is apparent when it is demonstrated.

Beyond and on the right again there are more examples of the

Hand boring machines were used for boring through the blocks and then cleaning or 'rincing' the bobbins

❖ THE MILL'S EXPANSION ❖

The Old Mill of 1835 was a two-storey rectangular building with an enclosed water-wheel pit at its northern end. At the southern end, a hearth and workshop were located in a separate adjunct, to reduce the risk of fire. Large rectangular windows on each side lit both floors to provide maximum light. The ground floor was given over to cutting and glueing; the upper floor housed the lathes, located on timber beds anchored to the outer walls. It was a compact, highly functional arrangement.

The period of expansion probably came after the mid-1860s when Elizabeth Coward and her son William took over the lease. The coppice barns are of a style which suggests this period, and the new, heavier lathes which were coming in would not have been suitable for the timber, upper floor of the Old Mill, so were housed in the more spacious New Lathe Shop where they could be anchored to the ground. It seems likely that the large, single storey lathe shop, the engine room and boiler house, with drying rooms above, the detached smithy, with its drying loft, and the coppice barns and cart shed (since demolished) were all completed by the 1880s.

The New Lathe Shop in the 1890s

Blocks being shaped on the roughing lathe

freestanding machines introduced in the late nineteenth century. They are **semi-automatic borers** made locally by the engineer Braithwaite of Crook, for smaller bobbins. Behind them are **finishing lathes**, one of which will be demonstrated, used to give the bobbins their final shape. These lathes were also made locally, by Fells of Troutbeck Bridge. Note the many small, sharp chisels that were fixed into the tool 'sets' to cut the timber. They all had to be kept sharp, and in good condition by the bobbin turner.

Among the clutter round the mill are swills. These are baskets made from sapling oak, boiled and split into strips and woven on a hazel hoop. They were used to carry blocks and bobbins around the mill. They were made in the mill yard, in sufficient numbers also to be sold in their own right

OLD LATHE SHOP

A stairway leads from the New Lathe Shop to the Old Lathe Shop, on the upper floor of the Old Mill. Before reaching the original production floor of the mill, you pass through an adjunct to the building, added to the Old Mill before the New Lathe Shop was built. It houses the tool room, with its grindstone and other equipment used by the bobbin turners to sharpen the tools and keep their machines working, and a hearth, used for the glue pot. It is because both these activities could start a fire that they are located outside the main mill building. As this room was the warmest in the mill, it also served as a mess room for the workpeople.

In the Old Lathe Shop, the stocks of the original lathes were mounted on the wooden beds ranged along beside the windows. Their weight was carried on the structure of the building, but they could not be set as

❖ BOBBIN TURNERS ❖

Bobbin turners were the workpeople who actually made the bobbins, by operating lathes on which the timber was shaped. At Stott Park during the nineteenth century those described as turners were generally men, and they carried out the finishing processes.

Among the workforce were young boys and teenage apprentices. The boys, some only eight years old, were employed for fetching and carrying and glueing the ends of the bobbins. The apprentices would carry out the roughing and rincing of the blocks.

In the 1860s Government inspectors' reports described

A young boy working the automatic boring machine c.1906

KENDAL LIBRARY, CUMBRIA COUNTY COUNCIL

the work as dangerous. Small pieces of timber could fly off the unguarded machines and cause injuries to the head or hands; and the atmosphere in the mill would have been heavy with sawdust which caused res- piratory diseases. Because there were not enough local people available, boys from work- houses in Lancashire were brought to work in the bobbin mills, where employment was not regulated until 1867.

precisely as the later lathes mounted on iron stands. This arrangement also gave maximum light for working. Power was transmitted from the waterwheel, behind the end wall, to the line shaft running through the apex of the roof among the timbers.

After the construction of the New Lathe Shop, the old shop was used for polishing, counting, weighing and dispatching. For this process, the bobbins were first placed on the wooden sieves to remove unwanted shavings, then placed with a lump of paraffin wax in a barrel, which was then revolved. Two polishing barrels are still in position.

Moving through the shop and turning to the left, there is a gallery which looks down into the New Lathe Shop, on the left, and into the Engine Room, to the right. The opening to the Engine Room is modern, but the gallery itself was important to give ready access to the line shafting and pulleys that served the various machines.

Left: This is how an early lathe would have been mounted

The polishing barrels

The Old Lathe Shop. The original lathes were fixed to the wooden beds beneath the windows

At the far end of the gallery, a door leads into one of the **Drying Rooms**, with their floors of perforated iron plates, in the upper part of the boiler house, above the boiler. The partial drying of the rough bobbins was extremely important; the wood was cut when wet, but was easier to finish when dry, so after being turned on the roughing lathe and before going to the finishing lathe, the roughs were placed on racks in various drying rooms round the mill. A great deal of drying accommodation was required to sustain production, and the loft of the detached Smithy was provided with a perforated iron floor for this purpose.

The guided tour of the mill ends at this point, returning to the ticket office via the stairs in the old mill.

The circular saw and its moving bed in use in 1906

THE MILL GROUNDS

Outside, from the mill yard, it is possible to explore the rest of the site. By taking the pathway between the coppice barns and turning to the left, you will see the stream, the source of the mill's power, and the reason for its location. Beyond the stream is a small plantation of coppice, which is now managed to provide wood for charcoal manufacture, using the large metal container, or retort, nearby.

On the left, against the upper part of the old mill, is a large machine relocated at Stott Park to provide an impression of equipment sold off at the time of closure. The **circular saw** with a moving bed was used for cutting trees into planks. It was not used for the bobbin making process, but a similar machine was located here to take power from the main line shafting. Note the iron **crane**, similar to one originally at Stott Park, to lift the timber. Stott Park had to diversify from bobbin manufacture to survive when the demand for bobbins fell.

Behind the large circular saw it is possible to gain the best view into the **wheelpit**. Originally built to house a wheel of about 24ft diameter, it now houses the Armfield turbine of 1931. The large iron pipe which carries the water to the turbine can be clearly seen, together with the pipe which carries the water away. The inlet pipe runs from a small header pond, now located on

❖ COPPICING ❖

The Lakeland landscape, and particularly the area around Stott Park, still retains extensive areas of coppiced woodland. Coppiced means 'grown for cutting' and the plantations contain specific tree species, including alder, ash, birch and willow, which are managed and harvested on a cycle varying from seven to fifteen years to produce long, straight poles. Bobbin wood was normally coppiced on a cycle of at least fifteen years. A well-managed acre of coppice could produce 10,000 poles at each cutting. The poles had many uses: as timber, which was turned on lathes to produce chair and table legs, tool handles and, of course, bobbins; for charcoal, a very pure fuel for the iron industry, and a raw material for the gunpowder industry; and for the bark, which was used to make swill baskets, barrel hoops, and in tanneries.

Coppice wood in the grounds of the mill, before cutting

private ground across the road from the mill. The header pond itself is served from the large reservoir up on the fell at High Dam (see below).

Before leaving the site, note the high black shed with louvred openings. This building has three floors, accessible by ladders, and was constructed to provide even more accommodation for drying the rough bobbins before they were finished. Behind the shed is a flooded area

which was the site of the pond for the old mill when the wheel was in use, between 1835 and the 1860s.

THE MILL'S SURROUNDINGS

High Dam

High Dam is 1.5 km from the mill and was an important feature contributing to the success of the mill. It can be reached by leaving the large

❖ POWER ❖

The raw materials found in the Lake District could be worked locally because the high rainfall and mountainous terrain sustained numerous fast-flowing streams. Water-powered blast furnaces and forges for iron-working, and mills for corn, gunpowder manufacture and bobbin turning, populated the many small valleys.

Initially, these mills used waterwheels, some of which, like that at Stott Park, were of very large diameter. During the later nineteenth century the more efficient water turbines became more common. A local firm, Gilkes of Kendal, was in the forefront of their development from 1881. Its predecessor company, Williamson Bros, supplied many installations, including the first turbine at Stott Park. This was installed in about 1858 to power the old mill.

The expansion at Stott Park called for more power, so the steam engine was added in 1880 to supplement the turbine. Built by Bradleys of

A drawing of Stott Park's water-wheel, believed to have been about 24ft in diameter. The wheel was served by a millpond to the north west, fed in turn by streams, one of which originated at High Dam. (Drawing by Peter Dunn)

Brighouse, it was capable of developing 30 horsepower. Steam power was rare in the Lake District because the nearest coalfield was on the northwest Cumbrian coast, and transport was poor. At Stott Park, however, the engine was fuelled by the timber by-products of the mill itself.

The original turbine may

have been replaced in the 1890s, probably simply because of wear and tear. The late nineteenth century was a period of considerable advance in turbine design and efficiency, and there would certainly have been a marginal increase in the power available from the new machine. However, its limitation would have been the water source itself, and we know that the bobbin masters went to some expense to secure a reliable supply. Certainly the combination of water and steam power was more than adequate for the wood turning processes in the mill, because two large external circular saws were also driven from the power train.

The twentieth century witnessed little change to these arrangements. The turbine was replaced in 1931 by the present machine, manufactured by Armfields of Ringwood, Hampshire and installed by the local firm of Wright, Heap and Westwood. In 1941 Barrow Corporation installed an electric motor.

High Dam, the large, artificial tarn that provided the water supply for the mill

upper car park, and crossing the road to take the footpath which follows the road towards Finsthwaite village. Before reaching the village a track, signposted High Dam, turns off to the right, through the trees. The path leads through plantations which were managed for many years as coppice woodland, although recently they have been neglected. However, it is still possible to see the characteristic poles of coppiced timber, of the type used in the mill.

The first pond to be reached is Low Dam, which held sufficient water for a limited period. A further walk brings you to High Dam. This is an extensive artificial tarn which is both functional and beautiful. It characterises the way in which the bobbin trade harnessed and sustained, but did not destroy, its impressive natural Lakeland setting. It also gives a good idea of the volume of water required to run a modest, water-powered factory.

Finsthwaite village

Returning from High Dam, it is a short walk into Finsthwaite village – turn right at the main road. John Coward's house, The Copse, now privately owned, is passed on the right. Within the village are workers' cottages and a shop, converted by the Coward family from buildings they bought from 1867 onwards.

The Copse, Finsthwaite, which was begun in 1901 and probably completed in 1902

HISTORY

BOBBINS AND THE TEXTILE INDUSTRY

The rapid growth of bobbin manufacture during the early part of the nineteenth century was driven by the mechanisation in the textile industry from the late eighteenth century onwards. It was the poet William Blake who, during this period, immortalised the term 'dark Satanic mills', in his poem *Jerusalem*. The buildings to which he referred were the burgeoning multi-storey cotton spinning mills, whose scale, as individual buildings, was greater than all but a few ecclesiastical buildings and great houses up to that time. A typical mill contained thousands of spindles on its mules, and each spindle needed

The growth of bobbin mills was initially to supply the cotton mills, each of which needed thousands of bobbins for its spinning mules

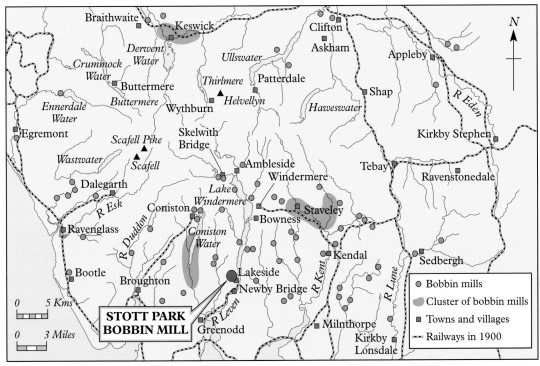

Bobbin mills in Lakeland

several bobbins to allow for continuous operation. At its height, just after 1900, the spinning town of Oldham had more than 20 million spindles in use in its numerous mills – equal to the whole spinning capacity of the United States at that time, and two-fifths of the United Kingdom total. Long before that, Lancashire's cotton industry had by far the most intensive concentration of textile manufacture anywhere in the world, and the Lakeland bobbin mills supplied its needs until other materials replaced wooden bobbins in the last quarter of the nineteenth century.

Bobbins are small wooden cylinders with ends to retain the yarn. However, when they are made there is a good deal of waste, so it was sensible to produce them near the source of the raw material, coppiced timber. As water, for power, was also abundant, the Lakeland industry was able to grow quickly.

The bobbin mills were not the first to use these resources: some were located where there had been ironworks, which had used water power to provide an air blast for their furnaces and coppiced wood for their fuel. We know from records that Stott Park was a new building, but it has never been established whether or not it was on a new site. The remains of some ironworking processes are not substantial, and the development of the bobbin mill over time could have obliterated them.

OWNERS OF THE MILL

The old mill building at Stott Park was built in 1835 by John Harrison, an independent landed farmer or yeoman. Typical of their class, the Harrisons had lived in Furness for many generations and they were well established socially and economically. In the seventeenth century they had inherited Low Stott Park Farm and the land around it. Later, the family moved into a substantial house, called The Landing, at Lakeside.

Neither John nor his youngest brother Myles, who inherited the estate on John's death, worked at or managed the mill. It was built as a speculative venture, and was advertised in the *Westmorland Gazette and Kendal Advertiser* on 5 December 1835 and 27 February 1836:

> This mill has been recently erected and is eligibly situated in Finsthwaite in the parish of Colton, Lancs., possessing sufficient convenience and power for thirty lathes [the earlier advertisement

Thomas Newby Wilson, who inherited the mill in 1867. He died in 1915

says twenty-four lathes; the increase in number may have been to make the mill seem more attractive] exclusive of all other appendages, together with a roomy and convenient dwelling house and an extensive garden and (if required by the taker) two or three cottages will be erected and be ready to be entered upon at the same time.

John Harrison died in 1843 and Myles in 1848. Myles's widow, Elizabeth, ran the estate for almost twenty years and on her death in 1867 the inheritance passed to Thomas Newby Wilson, her grandson. The estate was administered by trustees, however, and Newby Wilson, a typical late nineteenth-century gentleman, took little interest in it.

THE FIRST BOBBIN MASTERS

The first lessee of the mill was probably a Mr Rushford, and by 1839 he was in partnership with a man named Smith. By the time of the 1841 census, the lease was in the hands of James Bethom, who employed four journeymen, or turners, and six apprentices. One of these turners, William Wharton, a cousin of Bethom and son of Christopher Wharton, a bobbin master at Ings, near Staveley, took over the running of the mill in the late 1840s. However, he died young in 1855 at the age of 37, leaving four children. Such a premature death would not be

❖ LAKELAND ENTREPRENEURS ❖

Lakeland families from different social backgrounds took advantage of their ownership of land and commercial instincts to exploit the raw materials of the area and, some would say, the less fortunate members of the community. Many bobbin mills used buildings converted from other uses, among them blast furnaces, forges, corn and paper mills, because the owners considered the bobbin trade to be more profitable. The Harrisons who built Stott Park were of long-established, local farming stock who saw the bobbin trade as a commercial opportunity. They came from a quite different social background from the Cowards, who, like the previous lessees of the mill, were artisans. The Cowards were innkeepers and corn millers who came from Skelwith Bridge, to the north west of Lake Windermere.

Jeremiah Coward of Skelwith Bridge, whose relatives leased Stott Park mill from 1855 and oversaw the mill's expansion

unusual, as we know that working conditions in the mills led to consumption and dust-related disease.

On William Wharton's death the lease was immediately taken up by Thomas Eyers, a native of Kirkby Lonsdale who was formerly employed as a turner at the nearby Force Forge Mill. Eyers had married Susannah, the second daughter of Jeremiah Coward, owner of the Hare and Hound Inn (now the Skelwith Bridge Hotel) and corn mill at Skelwith Bridge. Following his marriage, Thomas worked at the Skelwith bobbin mill which the Cowards had set up in the 1830s. From the time Eyers took up the Stott Park lease, in 1855, the mill was continuously linked with the Coward family until its closure.

THE COWARD FAMILY

During the 1860s, Thomas and Susannah Eyers bought their own bobbin mill at Crooklands, and moved there. Jeremiah Coward was still alive (he died in 1871), and Elizabeth, the widow of his eldest son, and her son, William Coward, took on the Stott Park lease.

Their period of tenure saw many changes. The trade itself had been affected not only by the cotton famine, caused by the American Civil War, but also because traditional bobbins were less in demand, having been superseded by cardboard pirns (spools) and cops (spindles). Diversification was essential. At the same time, heavier, faster machines were available. These could produce not only one-piece bobbins more quickly, but also a range of other products, among them reels, implement handles and various types of shim (packing piece) and washer.

Many mills closed, but the Cowards responded by expanding, a decision influenced no doubt because,

❖ TRANSPORT ❖

Transport has always been difficult in Lakeland; some of the quickest and most efficient routes were those using the lakes themselves. The roads were, and are, sinuous and hilly. No canals or railways penetrate the heart of the area. We know little about transport in the early days of Stott Park. However, charcoal was transported extensively in the district for iron and gunpowder manufacture. The roads and tracks for carts and pack animals must therefore have been adequate for the sacks of bobbins. We know that the main routes were well served by carters who went far afield, including the textile towns of Lancashire.

After the arrival of the railway at Lakeside Station, which opened in 1869, and until its closure in 1964, the sacks of bobbins were taken by horse and cart and later by lorry to that station for onward transmission.

Furness Railway no. 20, built in 1863, at Lakeside Station

TIM OWEN/FURNESS RAILWAY TRUST

❖ LIVING CONDITIONS ❖

The Harrison family, the original owners of Stott Park, provided accommodation nearby for the bobbin master and his family to live in, but the nature of the workforce, which included boys and young unmarried men, meant that provision had to be made for them, too. So the house, in one of the buildings opposite the mill, was virtually a small hostel. Records show that those workers who were family men might walk many miles daily to work from their homes across the Fells.

As the nineteenth century progressed, the young men who stayed settled down and had families, so the bobbin masters, the Coward family, bought cottages for them to occupy, in Finsthwaite village nearby. However, these workers remained doubly tied, as the Cowards notoriously insisted that provisions were bought in their shop – at their prices.

Cottages in Finsthwaite, bought by the Coward family to accommodate the mill workers. (The cottages are now privately owned)

after 1869, they were so favourably situated in relation to the new railway terminus at Lakeside. They built a new lathe shop, and replaced the water-wheel with a turbine, later supplemented by a steam engine. New markets, as far afield as India, were sought out and supplied with a wide range of products.

The Coward family's investment was considerable, given that they did not own the mill. That was understandable, as the owning estate was run by trustees, and Thomas Newby Wilson took little interest in his lands or the mill, preferring the gentlemanly pursuits of sports and hunting. The Cowards on the other hand maintained a continuous interest, and apart from expanding the mill, they bought property to house their workers and land for coppicing.

Elizabeth Coward died in 1879 at the age of 62 and her son William only survived her by three years, dying at the age of 39. However, the lease was kept in the family, and was taken on by William's widow, in partnership with his younger brother John. For the next thirty years John rigidly controlled the mill and the community around it. Not only did he own the houses in which his workers lived, but his two sisters, Eliza and Margaret, also ran the shop where the workmen were expected to purchase their provisions. He oversaw this community from his newly built house, The Copse.

John married late and died childless in 1917. The mill passed back to William's surviving son, also named John, who bought the mill from the surviving trustees of the estate in 1921 for £4000. John Coward ran the mill until his death in 1954, but the family's interest in the community was greatly diminished in the 1930s when they moved to Cartmel Fell. From 1954 until Stott Park's closure in 1971 the business was in the hands of John's son, Bobby Coward. He took into partnership Jack Ivison, who had worked at Stott Park since the 1920s. Jack, who managed the mill in its declining years, and continued to live locally until his death in 1986, contributed greatly in his retirement to the under-standing of the bobbin industry, the working of the mill, and therefore to this narrative.

THE WORKPEOPLE

The mill at Stott Park sustained a small community for almost a century and a half, and the continuity of man-agement by the extended Coward family was mirrored by a similar con-tinuity among the bobbin turners.

Fifteen to twenty-five men and boys were constantly kept in employment at Stott Park for about a century from the 1860s. Many of the early workers were incomers, including youngsters from workhouses, but by 1900 there was a settled workforce.

A good deal is known about some of the individual families. Charles Jackson is recorded on the 1841 census as an apprentice at the mill, then aged 'over fifteen'. He had been born in either Windermere or Ambleside. In 1848 he married a local girl named Anne Fell, and they had six children. In the 1860s this family lived in one of the Plum Green Cottages in Finsthwaite, where Anne ran a shop. The eldest of their surviving sons became a bobbin turner but died at the age of 35; his father survived until 1907, dying at the age of 82.

Another bobbin turner was John Lewis, who was born in Backbarrow. His son, Robert, also became a turner and eventually foreman at the mill. Of his three daughters Mary married Nathan Whitehead, a bobbin turner, and Eleanor was married twice: first to a bobbin turner and secondly to a sawyer. At various times during the Coward era, the mill employed the father, brother, brother-in-law, both husbands, one son, two sons-in-law and two grandchildren of Eleanor Lewis.

At work on the finishing lathes c.1906. On the left is James Gibson, and on the right is James Hodgson, one of the many relatives of Eleanor Lewis who worked at the mill

NEW PRODUCTS

The demand for bobbins for the textile trade, which had boomed during the earlier part of the nineteenth century, diminished almost as quickly from the 1860s. Many mills went out of business. Those which survived, like Stott Park, diversified and the demand for new products enabled them to expand and re-equip. Among the new products were bobbins for sewing cotton and thread, and for wire, but the detailed order books that survive for the period 1908–21 indicate a high volume a production of other items. These included tool handles, particularly for files and mallets; shafts for picks, hammers and axes; spade crowns; duffle-coat toggles and spout bobbins. The spout bobbin was the small round wooden washer which fitted between a wall and a drainpipe bracket, and the many thousands produced were a staple of Stott Park's trade. The raw materials remained largely the same throughout. Handles were turned from ash, bobbins from birch. Occasionally hickory was used for pick handles, and this would have been sourced from abroad.

A selection of bobbins and other turned wood products, made when the mill diversified

CLOSURE

It was the introduction of plastic reels, handles and bobbins which finally brought about the mill's demise. Its closure and sale to the Department of the Environment in 1971 saw the end of what had been a steadily declining connection between the mill owners and the local community. Bobby Coward died in 1978, and the remaining properties owned by the family in Finsthwaite were sold off over the years.

The bobbin industry had been an intrinsic part of the area's economy, and Stott Park was one of the last bobbin mills to close in the Lake District. The Department of the Environment reopened the mill as a working museum in 1983, and it passed into the care of English Heritage in 1984. The mill which you see today, scarcely different in appearance from a century ago, stands as a unique monument to a once thriving and vital industry.

ACKNOWLEDGEMENTS

In a series of books, Dr John Marshall and Mr Michael Davies-Shiel first brought the Lakeland bobbin industry to the attention of a wider public in the 1960s and they have both generously continued to provide information from their researches. Over a similar period, Mrs Janet Martin has most kindly advised on many matters relating to the history of the locality, and particularly its families. The assistance of the late Mr Jack Ivison of Finsthwaite, who spent almost the whole of his adult life at the mill, was crucial to an understanding both of the way in which Stott Park worked, and of the industry generally. My former colleague Ian Ayris, who also assisted with this text, undertook further research and expertly collated the substantial volume of material generated by the Stott Park project. Mike Nield, currently the manager of the mill, made a valuable contribution during the drafting of this text, as has Paul Pattison in subsequent revisions.